Frances Ellen Watkins Harper

Poems

Frances Ellen Watkins Harper

Poems

ISBN/EAN: 9783741114861

Manufactured in Europe, USA, Canada, Australia, Japa

Cover: Foto ©Andreas Hilbeck / pixelio.de

Manufactured and distributed by brebook publishing software (www.brebook.com)

Frances Ellen Watkins Harper

Poems

Frances Ellen Watkins Harper

Poems

POEMS

BY

FRANCES E. W. HARPER

PHILADELPHIA:
1006 BAINBRIDGE STREET
1896

Whereas thou hast been forsaken and hated, so that no man went through thee, I will make thee an eternal excellency, a joy of many generations.— ISAIAH 60 : 15.

1006 Bainbridge Street,
Philadelphia, Pa.

CONTENTS.

	PAGE
My Mother's Kiss	1
A Grain of Sand	3
The Crocuses	4
The Present Age	6
Dedication Poem	9
A Double Standard	12
Our Hero	15
The Dying Bondman	17
A Little Child Shall Lead Them	19
The Sparrow's Fall	21
God Bless Our Native Land	23
Dandelions	24
The Building	25
Home, Sweet Home	26
The Pure in Heart Shall See God	28
He Had Not Where to Lay His Head	30
Go Work in My Vineyard	31
Renewal of Strength	33
Jamie's Puzzle	34
Truth	36
Death of the Old Sea King	38
Save the Boys	40

CONTENTS.

	PAGE
Nothing and Something	42
Vashti	44
Thank God for Little Children	47
The Martyr of Alabama	49
The Night of Death	53
Mother's Treasures	56
The Refiner's Gold	58
A Story of the Rebellion	60
Burial of Sarah	61
Going East	63
The Hermit's Sacrifice	66
Songs for the People	69
Let the Light Enter	71
An Appeal to My Country Women	72

My Mother's Kiss.

My mother's kiss, my mother's kiss,
   I feel its impress now;
As in the bright and happy days
   She pressed it on my brow.

You say it is a fancied thing
   Within my memory fraught;
To me it has a sacred place—
   The treasure house of thought.

Again, I feel her fingers glide
   Amid my clustering hair;
I see the love-light in her eyes,
   When all my life was fair.

Again, I hear her gentle voice
   In warning or in love.
How precious was the faith that taught
   My soul of things above.

The music of her voice is stilled,
  Her lips are paled in death.
As precious pearls I'll clasp her words
  Until my latest breath.

The world has scattered round my path
  Honor and wealth and fame;
But naught so precious as the thoughts
  That gather round her name.

And friends have placed upon my brow
  The laurels of renown;
But she first taught me how to wear
  My manhood as a crown.

My hair is silvered o'er with age,
  I'm longing to depart;
To clasp again my mother's hand,
  And be a child at heart.

To roam with her the glory-land
  Where saints and angels greet;
To cast our crowns with songs of love
  At our Redeemer's feet.

A Grain of Sand.

Do you see this grain of sand
Lying loosely in my hand?
Do you know to me it brought
Just a simple loving thought?
When one gazes night by night
On the glorious stars of light,
Oh how little seems the span
Measured round the life of man.

Oh! how fleeting are his years
With their smiles and their tears;
Can it be that God does care
For such atoms as we are?
Then outspake this grain of sand
" I was fashioned by His hand
In the star lit realms of space
I was made to have a place.

" Should the ocean flood the world,
Were its mountains 'gainst me hurled,
All the force they could employ
Wouldn't a single grain destroy;
And if I, a thing so light,
Have a place within His sight;
You are linked unto his throne
Cannot live nor die alone.

In the everlasting arms
Mid life's dangers and alarms
Let calm trust your spirit fill;
Know He's God, and then be still."
Trustingly I raised my head
Hearing what the atom said;
Knowing man is greater far
Than the brightest sun or star.

The Crocuses.

They heard the South wind sighing
  A murmur of the rain;
And they knew that Earth was longing
  To see them all again.

While the snow-drops still were sleeping
  Beneath the silent sod;
They felt their new life pulsing
  Within the dark, cold clod.

Not a daffodil nor daisy
  Had dared to raise its head;
Not a fairhaired dandelion
  Peeped timid from its bed;

THE CROCUSES.

Though a tremor of the winter
   Did shivering through them run;
Yet they lifted up their foreheads
   To greet the vernal sun.

And the sunbeams gave them welcome,
   As did the morning air—
And scattered o'er their simple robes
   Rich tints of beauty rare.

Soon a host of lovely flowers
   From vales and woodland burst;
But in all that fair procession
   The crocuses were first.

First to weave for Earth a chaplet
   To crown her dear old head;
And to beautify the pathway
   Where winter still did tread.

And their loved and white haired mother
   Smiled sweetly 'neath the touch,
When she knew her faithful children
   Were loving her so much.

The Present Age.

Say not the age is hard and cold—
I think it brave and grand;
When men of diverse sects and creeds
Are clasping hand in hand.

The Parsee from his sacred fires
Beside the Christian kneels;
And clearer light to Islam's eyes
The word of Christ reveals.

The Brahmin from his distant home
Brings thoughts of ancient lore;
The Bhuddist breaking bonds of caste
Divides mankind no more.

The meek-eyed sons of far Cathay
Are welcome round the board;
Not greed, nor malice drives away
These children of our Lord.

And Judah from whose trusted hands
Came oracles divine;
Now sits with those around whose hearts
The light of God doth shine.

THE PRESENT AGE.

Japan unbars her long sealed gates
   From islands far away;
Her sons are lifting up their eyes
   To greet the coming day.

The Indian child from forests wild
   Has learned to read and pray;
The tomahawk and scalping knife
   From him have passed away.

From centuries of servile toil
   The Negro finds release,
And builds the fanes of prayer and praise
   Unto the God of Peace.

England and Russia face to face
   With Central Asia meet;
And on the far Pacific coast,
   Chinese and natives greet.

Crusaders once with sword and shield
   The Holy Land to save;
From Moslem hands did strive to clutch
   The dear Redeemer's grave.

A battle greater, grander far
   Is for the present age;

A crusade for the rights of man
  To brighten history's page.

Where labor faints and bows her head,
  And want consorts with crime;
Or men grown faithless sadly say
  That evil is the time.

There is the field, the vantage ground
  For every earnest heart;
To side with justice, truth and right
  And act a noble part.

To save from ignorance and vice
  The poorest, humblest child;
To make our age the fairest one
  On which the sun has smiled;

To plant the roots of coming years
  In mercy, love and truth;
And bid our weary, saddened earth
  Again renew her youth.

Oh! earnest hearts! toil on in hope,
  'Till darkness shrinks from light;
To fill the earth with peace and joy,
  Let youth and age unite;

To stay the floods of sin and shame
  That sweep from shore to shore;
And furl the banners stained with blood,
  'Till war shall be no more.

Blame not the age, nor think it full
  Of evil and unrest;
But say of every other age,
  " This one shall be the best."

The age to brighten every path
  By sin and sorrow trod;
For loving hearts to usher in
  The commonwealth of God.

DEDICATION POEM.

Dedication Poem on the reception of the annex to the home for aged colored people, from the bequest of Mr. Edward T. Parker.

Outcast from her home in Syria
  In the lonely, dreary wild;
Heavy hearted, sorrow stricken,
  Sat a mother and her child.

There was not a voice to cheer her
  Not a soul to share her fate;
She was weary, he was fainting,—
  And life seemed so desolate.

Far away in sunny Egypt
  Was lone Hagar's native land;
Where the Nile in kingly bounty
  Scatters bread with gracious hand.

In the tents of princely Abram
  She for years had found a home;
Till the stern decree of Sarah
  Sent her forth the wild to roam.

Hour by hour she journeyed onward
  From the shelter of their tent,
Till her footsteps slowly faltered
  And the water all was spent;

Then she veiled her face in sorrow,
  Feared her child would die of thirst;
Till her eyes with tears so holden
  Saw a sparkling fountain burst.

Oh! how happy was that mother,
  What a soothing of her pain;

DEDICATION POEM.

When she saw her child reviving,
  Life rejoicing through each vein

Does not life repeat this story,
  Tell it over day by day?
Of the fountains of refreshment
  Ever springing by our way.

Here is one by which we gather,
  On this bright and happy day,
Just to bask beside a fountain
  Making gladder life's highway.

Bringing unto hearts now aged
  Who have borne life's burdens long,
Such a gift of love and mercy
  As deserves our sweetest song.

Such a gift that even heaven
  May rejoice with us below,
If the pure and holy angels
  Join us in our joy and woe.

May the memory of the giver
  In this home where age may rest,
Float like fragrance through the ages,
  Ever blessing, ever blest.

When the gates of pearl are opened
  May we there this friend behold,
Drink with him from living fountains,
  Walk with him the streets of gold.

When life's shattered cords of music
  Shall again be sweetly sung;
Then our hearts with life immortal,
  Shall be young, forever young.

A Double Standard.

Do you blame me that I loved him?
  If when standing all alone
I cried for bread a careless world
  Pressed to my lips a stone.

Do you blame me that I loved him,
  That my heart beat glad and free,
When he told me in the sweetest tones
  He loved but only me?

Can you blame me that I did not see
  Beneath his burning kiss
The serpent's wiles, nor even hear
  The deadly adder hiss?

A DOUBLE STANDARD.

Can you blame me that my heart grew cold
   That the tempted, tempter turned;
When he was feted and caressed
   And I was coldly spurned?

Would you blame him, when you draw from
   me
   Your dainty robes aside,
If he with gilded baits should claim
   Your fairest as his bride?

Would you blame the world if it should press
   On him a civic crown;
And see me struggling in the depth
   Then harshly press me down?

Crime has no sex and yet to-day
   I wear the brand of shame;
Whilst he amid the gay and proud
   Still bears an honored name.

Can you blame me if I've learned to think
   Your hate of vice a sham,
When you so coldly crushed me down
   And then excused the man?

Would you blame me if to-morrow
   The coroner should say,

A wretched girl, outcast, forlorn,
  Has thrown her life away?

Yes, blame me for my downward course,
  But oh! remember well,
Within your homes you press the hand
  That led me down to hell.

I'm glad God's ways are not our ways,
  He does not see as man;
Within His love I know there's room
  For those whom others ban.

I think before His great white throne,
  His throne of spotless light,
That whited sepulchres shall wear
  The hue of endless night.

That I who fell, and he who sinned,
  Shall reap as we have sown;
That each the burden of his loss
  Must bear and bear alone.

No golden weights can turn the scale
  Of justice in His sight;
And what is wrong in woman's life
  In man's cannot be right.

Our Hero.

Onward to her destination,
   O'er the stream the Hannah sped,
When a cry of consternation
   Smote and chilled our hearts with dread.

Wildly leaping, madly sweeping,
   All relentless in their sway,
Like a band of cruel demons
   Flames were closing 'round our way

Oh! the horror of those moments;
   Flames above and waves below—
Oh! the agony of ages
   Crowded in one hour of woe.

Fainter grew our hearts with anguish
   In that hour with peril rife,
When we saw the pilot flying,
   Terror-stricken, for his life.

Then a man uprose before us—
   We had once despised his race—
But we saw a lofty purpose
   Lighting up his darkened face.

While the flames were madly roaring,
　　With a courage grand and high,
Forth he rushed unto our rescue,
　　Strong to suffer, brave to die.

Helplessly the boat was drifting,
　　Death was staring in each face,
When he grasped the fallen rudder,
　　Took the pilot's vacant place.

Could he save us? Would he save us?
　　All his hope of life give o'er?
Could he hold that fated vessel
　　'Till she reached the nearer shore?

All our hopes and fears were centered
　　'Round his strong, unfaltering hand;
If he failed us we must perish,
　　Perish just in sight of land.

Breathlessly we watched and waited
　　While the flames were raging fast;
When our anguish changed to rapture—
　　We were saved, yes, saved at last.

Never strains of sweetest music
　　Brought to us more welcome sound

Than the grating of that steamer
  When her keel had touched the ground.

But our faithful martyr hero
  Through a fiery pathway trod,
Till he laid his valiant spirit
  On the bosom of his God.

Fame has never crowned a hero
  On the crimson fields of strife,
Grander, nobler, than that pilot
  Yielding up for us his life.

———

The Dying Bondman.

Life was trembling, faintly trembling
On the bondman's latest breath,
And he felt the chilling pressure
Of the cold, hard hand of Death.

He had been an Afric chieftain,
Worn his manhood as a crown;
But upon the field of battle
Had been fiercely stricken down.

He had longed to gain his freedom,
Waited, watched and hoped in vain,
Till his life was slowly ebbing—
Almost broken was his chain.

By his bedside stood the master,
Gazing on the dying one,
Knowing by the dull grey shadows
That life's sands were almost run.

" Master," said the dying bondman,
" Home and friends I soon shall see;
But before I reach my country,
Master write that I am free;

" For the spirits of my fathers
Would shrink back from me in pride,
If I told them at our greeting
I a slave had lived and died;—

" Give to me the precious token,
That my kindred dead may see—
Master! write it, write it quickly!
Master! write that I am free!"

At his earnest plea the master
Wrote for him the glad release,

O'er his wan and wasted features
Flitted one sweet smile of peace.

Eagerly he grasped the writing;
"I am free!" at last he said.
Backward fell upon the pillow,
He was free among the dead.

"A Little Child Shall Lead Them."

Only a little scrap of blue
   Preserved with loving care,
But earth has not a brilliant hue
   To me more bright and fair.

Strong drink, like a raging demon,
   Laid on my heart his hand,
When my darling joined with others
   The Loyal Legion * band.

But mystic angels called away
   My loved and precious child,
And o'er life's dark and stormy way
   Swept waves of anguish wild.

* The Temperance Band,

This badge of the Loyal Legion
  We placed upon her breast,
As she lay in her little coffin
  Taking her last sweet rest.

To wear that badge as a token
  She earnestly did crave,
So we laid it on her bosom
  To wear it in the grave.

Where sorrow would never reach her
  Nor harsh words smite her ear;
Nor her eyes in death dimmed slumber
  Would ever shed a tear.

" What means this badge? " said her father,
  Whom we had tried to save;
Who said, when we told her story,
  " Don't put it in the grave."

We took the badge from her bosom
  And laid it on a chair;
And men by drink deluded
  Knelt by that badge in prayer.

And vowed in that hour of sorrow
  From drink they would abstain;

And this little badge became the wedge
Which broke their galling chain.

And lifted the gloomy shadows
   That overspread my life,
And flooding my home with gladness,
   Made me a happy wife.

And this is why this scrap of blue
   Is precious in my sight;
It changed my sad and gloomy home
   From darkness into light.

The Sparrow's Fall.

Too frail to soar—a feeble thing—
It fell to earth with fluttering wing;
But God, who watches over all,
Beheld that little sparrow's fall.

'Twas not a bird with plumage gay,
Filling the air with its morning lay;
'Twas not an eagle bold and strong,
Borne on the tempest's wing along.

Only a brown and weesome thing,
With drooping head and listless wing;
It could not drift beyond His sight
Who marshals the splendid stars of night.

Its dying chirp fell on His ears,
Who tunes the music of the spheres,
Who hears the hungry lion's call,
And spreads a table for us all.

Its mission of song at last is done,
No more will it greet the rising sun;
That tiny bird has found a rest
More calm than its mother's downy breast.

Oh, restless heart, learn thou to trust
In God, so tender, strong and just;
In whose love and mercy everywhere
His humblest children have a share.

If in love He numbers ev'ry hair,
Whether the strands be dark or fair,
Shall we not learn to calmly rest,
Like children, on our Father's breast?

God Bless Our Native Land.

God bless our native land,
   Land of the newly free,
Oh may she ever stand
   For truth and liberty.

God bless our native land,
   Where sleep our kindred dead,
Let peace at thy command
   Above their graves be shed.

God help our native land,
   Bring surcease to her strife,
And shower from thy hand
   A more abundant life.

God bless our native land,
   Her homes and children bless,
Oh may she ever stand
   For truth and righteousness.

DANDELIONS.

Welcome children of the Spring,
   In your garbs of green and gold,
Lifting up your sun-crowned heads
   On the verdant plain and wold.

As a bright and joyous troop
   From the breast of earth ye came
Fair and lovely are your cheeks,
   With sun-kisses all aflame.

In the dusty streets and lanes,
   Where the lowly children play,
There as gentle friends ye smile,
   Making brighter life's highway.

Dewdrops and the morning sun,
   Weave your garments fair and bright,
And we welcome you to-day
   As the children of the light.

Children of the earth and sun,
   We are slow to understand
All the richness of the gifts
   Flowing from our Father's hand.

Were our vision clearer far,
   In this sin-dimmed world of ours,
Would we not more thankful be
   For the love that sends us flowers?

Welcome, early visitants,
   With your sun-crowned golden hair,
With your message to our hearts
   Of our Father's loving care.

The Building.

"Build me a house," said the Master,
   "But not on the shifting sand,
Mid the wreck and roar of tempests,
   A house that will firmly stand.

"I will bring thee windows of agates,
   And gates of carbuncles bright,
And thy fairest courts and portals
   Shall be filled with love and light.

"Thou shalt build with fadeless rubies,
   All fashioned around the throne,
A house that shall last forever,
   With Christ as the cornerstone.

"It shall be a royal mansion,
  A fair and beautiful thing,
It will be the presence-chamber
  Of thy Saviour, Lord and King.

"Thy house shall be bound with pinions
  To mansions of rest above,
But grace shall forge all the fetters
  With the links and cords of love.

"Thou shalt be free in this mansion
  From sorrow and pain of heart,
For the peace of God shall enter,
  And never again depart."

Home, Sweet Home.

Sharers of a common country,
  They had met in deadly strife;
Men who should have been as brothers
  Madly sought each other's life.

In the silence of the even,
  When the cannon's lips were dumb,

Thoughts of home and all its loved ones
  To the soldier's heart would come.

On the margin of a river,
  'Mid the evening's dews and damps,
Could be heard the sounds of music
  Rising from two hostile camps.

One was singing of its section
  Down in Dixie, Dixie's land,
And the other of the banner
  Waved so long from strand to strand.

In the land where Dixie's ensign
  Floated o'er the hopeful slave,
Rose the song that freedom's banner,
  Starry-lighted, long might wave.

From the fields of strife and carnage,
  Gentle thoughts began to roam,
And a tender strain of music
  Rose with words of " Home, Sweet Home.'

Then the hearts of strong men melted,
  For amid our grief and sin
Still remains that "touch of nature,"
  Telling us we all are kin.

In one grand but gentle chorus,
  Floating to the starry dome,
Came the words that brought them nearer.
  Words that told of "Home, Sweet Home."

For awhile, all strife forgotten,
  They were only brothers then,
Joining in the sweet old chorus,
  Not as soldiers, but as men.

Men whose hearts would flow together,
  Though apart their feet might roam,
Found a tie they could not sever,
  In the mem'ry of each home.

Never may the steps of carnage
  Shake our land from shore to shore,
But may mother, home and Heaven,
  Be our watchwords evermore.

THE PURE IN HEART SHALL SEE GOD.

They shall see Him in the crimson flush
  Of morning's early light,
In the drapery of sunset,
  Around the couch of night.

THE PURE IN HEART SHALL SEE GOD.

When the clouds drop down their fatness,
    In late and early rain,
They shall see His glorious footprints
    On valley, hill and plain.

They shall see Him when the cyclone
    Breathes terror through the land;
They shall see Him 'mid the murmurs
    Of zephyrs soft and bland.

They shall see Him when the lips of health,
    Breath vigor through each nerve,
When pestilence clasps hands with death,
    His purposes to serve.

They shall see Him when the trembling earth
    Is rocking to and fro;
They shall see Him in the order
    The seasons come and go.

They shall see Him when the storms of war
    Sweep wildly through the land;
When peace descends like gentle dew
    They still shall see His hand.

They shall see Him in the city
    Of gems and pearls of light,

They shall see Him in his beauty,
    And walk with Him in white.

To living founts their feet shall tend,
    And Christ shall be their guide,
Beloved of God, their rest shall be
    In safety by His side.

He "Had Not Where to Lay His Head."

The conies had their hiding-place,
    The wily fox with stealthy tread
A covert found, but Christ, the Lord,
    Had not a place to lay his head.

The eagle had an eyrie home,
    The blithesome bird its quiet rest,
But not the humblest spot on earth
    Was by the Son of God possessed.

Princes and kings had palaces,
    With grandeur could adorn each tomb,
For Him who came with love and life,
    They had no home, they gave no room.

The hands whose touch sent thrills of joy
  Through nerves unstrung and palsied
    frame,
The feet that travelled for our need,
  Were nailed unto the cross of shame.

How dare I murmur at my lot,
  Or talk of sorrow, pain and loss,
When Christ was in a manger laid,
  And died in anguish on the cross.

That homeless one beheld beyond
  His lonely agonizing pain,
A love outflowing from His heart,
  That all the wandering world would gain.

Go Work in My Vineyard.

Go work in my vineyard, said the Lord,
  And gather the bruised grain;
But the reapers had left the stubble bare,
  And I trod the soil in pain.

The fields of my Lord are wide and broad,
  He has pastures fair and green,
And vineyards that drink the golden light
  Which flows from the sun's bright sheen.

I heard the joy of the reapers' song,
  As they gathered golden grain;
Then wearily turned unto my task,
  With a lonely sense of pain.

Sadly I turned from the sun's fierce glare,
  And sought the quiet shade,
And over my dim and weary eyes
  Sleep's peaceful fingers strayed.

I dreamed I joined with a restless throng,
  Eager for pleasure and gain;
But ever and anon a stumbler fell,
  And uttered a cry of pain.

But the eager crowd still hurried on,
  Too busy to pause or heed,
When a voice rang sadly through my soul,
  You must staunch these wounds that bleed.

My hands were weak, but I reached them out
  To feebler ones than mine,

And over the shadows of my life
   Stole the light of a peace divine.

Oh! then my task was a sacred thing,
   How precious it grew in my eyes!
'Twas mine to gather the bruised grain
   For the "Lord of Paradise."

And when the reapers shall lay their grain
   On the floors of golden light,
I feel that mine with its broken sheaves
   Shall be precious in His sight.

Though thorns may often pierce my feet,
   And the shadows still abide,
The mists will vanish before His smile,
   There will be light at eventide.

Renewal of Strength.

The prison-house in which I live
   Is falling to decay,
But God renews my spirit's strength,
   Within these walls of clay.

For me a dimness slowly creeps
  Around earth's fairest light,
But heaven grows clearer to my view,
  And fairer to my sight.

It may be earth's sweet harmonies
  Are duller to my ear,
But music from my Father's house
  Begins to float more near.

Then let the pillars of my home
  Crumble and fall away;
Lo, God's dear love within my soul
  Renews it day by day.

Jamie's Puzzle.

There was grief within our household
  Because of a vacant chair.
Our mother, so loved and precious,
  No longer was sitting there.

JAMIE'S PUZZLE.

Our hearts grew heavy with sorrow,
    Our eyes with tears were blind,
And little Jamie was wondering,
    Why we were left behind.

We had told our little darling,
    Of the land of love and light,
Of the saints all crowned with glory,
    And enrobed in spotless white.

We said that our precious mother,
    Had gone to that land so fair,
To dwell with beautiful angels,
    And to be forever there.

But the child was sorely puzzled,
    Why dear grandmamma should go
To dwell in a stranger city,
    When her children loved her so.

But again the mystic angel
    Came with swift and silent tread,
And our sister, Jamie's mother,
    Was enrolled among the dead.

To us the mystery deepened,
    To Jamie it seemed more clear;

Grandma, he said, must be lonesome,
And mamma has gone to her.

But the question lies unanswered
In our little Jamie's mind,
Why she should go to our mother,
And leave her children behind;

To dwell in that lovely city,
From all that was dear to part,
From children who loved to nestle
So closely around her heart.

Dear child, like you, we are puzzled,
With problems that still remain;
But think in the great hereafter
Their meaning will all be plain.

Truth.

A rock, for ages, stern and high,
Stood frowning 'gainst the earth and sky,
And never bowed his haughty crest
When angry storms around him prest.
Morn, springing from the arms of night,
Had often bathed his brow with light,

And kissed the shadows from his face
With tender love and gentle grace.

Day, pausing at the gates of rest,
Smiled on him from the distant West,
And from her throne the dark-browed Night
Threw round his path her softest light.
And yet he stood unmoved and proud,
Nor love, nor wrath, his spirit bowed;
He bared his brow to every blast
And scorned the tempest as it passed.

One day a tiny, humble seed—
The keenest eye would hardly heed—
Fell trembling at that stern rock's base,
And found a lowly hiding-place.
A ray of light, and drop of dew,
Came with a message, kind and true;
They told her of the world so bright,
Its love, its joy, and rosy light,
And lured her from her hiding-place,
To gaze upon earth's glorious face.

So, peeping timid from the ground,
She clasped the ancient rock around,
And climbing up with childish grace,
She held him with a close embrace;

Her clinging was a thing of dread;
Where'er she touched a fissure spread,
And he who'd breasted many a storm
Stood frowning there, a mangled form;
A Truth, dropped in the silent earth,
May seem a thing of little worth,
Till, spreading round some mighty wrong,
It saps its pillars proud and strong,
And o'er the fallen ruin weaves
The brightest blooms and fairest leaves.

DEATH OF THE OLD SEA KING.

'Twas a fearful night—the tempest raved
  With loud and wrathful pride,
The storm-king harnessed his lightning steeds,
  And rode on the raging tide.

The sea-king lay on his bed of death,
  Pale mourners around him bent;
They knew the wild and fitful life
  Of their chief was almost spent.

His ear was growing dull in death
  When the angry storm he heard,

The sluggish blood in the old man's veins
  With sudden vigor stirred.

" I hear them call," cried the dying man,
  His eyes grew full of light;
" Now bring me here my warrior robes,
  My sword and armor bright.

" In the tempest's lull I heard a voice,
  I knew 'twas Odin's call.
The Valkyrs are gathering round my bed
  To lead me unto his hall.

" Bear me unto my noblest ship,
  Light up a funeral pyre;
I'll walk to the palace of the braves
  Through a path of flame and fire."

Oh! wild and bright was the stormy light
  That flashed from the old man's eye,
As they bore him from the couch of death
  To his battle-ship to die,

And lit with many a mournful torch
  The sea-king's dying bed,
And like a banner fair and bright
  The flames around him spread.

But they heard no cry of anguish
    Break through that fiery wall,
With rigid brow and silent lips
    He was seeking Odin's hall.

Through a path of fearful splendor,
    While strong men held their breath,
The brave old man went boldly forth
    And calmly talked with death.

Save the Boys.

Like Dives in the deeps of Hell
I cannot break this fearful spell,
Nor quench the fires I've madly nursed,
Nor cool this dreadful raging thirst.
Take back your pledge—ye come too late!
Ye cannot save me from my fate,
Nor bring me back departed joys;
But ye can try to save the boys.

Ye bid me break my fiery chain,
Arise and be a man again,

When every street with snares is spread,
And nets of sin where'er I tread.
No; I must reap as I did sow.
The seeds of sin bring crops of woe;
But with my latest breath I'll crave
That ye will try the boys to save.

These bloodshot eyes were once so bright;
This sin-crushed heart was glad and light;
But by the wine-cup's ruddy glow
I traced a path to shame and woe.
A captive to my galling chain,
I've tried to rise, but tried in vain—
The cup allures and then destroys.
Oh! from its thraldom save the boys.

Take from your streets those traps of hell
Into whose gilded snares I fell.
Oh! freemen, from these foul decoys
Arise, and vote to save the boys.
Oh, ye who license men to trade
In draughts that charm and then degrade,
Before ye hear the cry, Too late,
Oh, save the boys from my sad fate.

Nothing and Something.

It is nothing to me, the beauty said,
With a careless toss of her pretty head;
The man is weak if he can't refrain
From the cup you say is fraught with pain.
It was something to her in after years,
When her eyes were drenched with burning tears,
And she watched in lonely grief and dread,
And startled to hear a staggering tread.

It is nothing to me, the mother said;
I have no fear that my boy will tread
In the downward path of sin and shame,
And crush my heart and darken his name.
It was something to her when that only son
From the path of right was early won,
And madly cast in the flowing bowl
A ruined body and sin-wrecked soul.

It is nothing to me, the young man cried:
In his eye was a flash of scorn and pride;
I heed not the dreadful things ye tell:
I can rule myself I know full well.

It was something to him when in prison he lay
The victim of drink, life ebbing away;
And thought of his wretched child and wife,
And the mournful wreck of his wasted life.

It is nothing to me, the merchant said,
As over his ledger he bent his head;
I'm busy to-day with tare and tret,
And I have no time to fume and fret.
It was something to him when over the wire
A message came from a funeral pyre—
A drunken conductor had wrecked a train,
And his wife and child were among the slain.

It is nothing to me, the voter said,
The party's loss is my greatest dread;
Then gave his vote for the liquor trade,
Though hearts were crushed and drunkards made.
It was something to him in after life,
When his daughter became a drunkard's wife
And her hungry children cried for bread,
And trembled to hear their father's tread.

Is it nothing for us to idly sleep
While the cohorts of death their vigils keep?
To gather the young and thoughtless in,
And grind in our midst a grist of sin?

It is something, yes, all, for us to stand
Clasping by faith our Saviour's hand;
To learn to labor, live and fight
On the side of God and changeless light.

Vashti.

She leaned her head upon her hand
    And heard the King's decree—
"My lords are feasting in my halls;
    Bid Vashti come to me.

"I've shown the treasures of my house,
    My costly jewels rare,
But with the glory of her eyes
    No rubies can compare.

"Adorn'd and crown'd I'd have her come,
    With all her queenly grace,
And, 'mid my lords and mighty men,
    Unveil her lovely face.

"Each gem that sparkles in my crown,
    Or glitters on my throne,

Grows poor and pale when she appears,
  My beautiful, my own!"

All waiting stood the chamberlains
  To hear the Queen's reply.
They saw her cheek grow deathly pale,
  But light flash'd to her eye:

"Go, tell the King," she proudly said,
  "That I am Persia's Queen,
And by his crowds of merry men
  I never will be seen.

"I'll take the crown from off my head
  And tread it 'neath my feet,
Before their rude and careless gaze
  My shrinking eyes shall meet.

"A queen unveil'd before the crowd!—
  Upon each lip my name!—
Why, Persia's women all would blush
  And weep for Vashti's shame!

"Go back!" she cried, and waved her hand,
  And grief was in her eye:
"Go, tell the King," she sadly said,
  "That I would rather die."

They brought her message to the King;
　　Dark flash'd his angry eye;
'Twas as the lightning ere the storm
　　Hath swept in fury by.

Then bitterly outspoke the King,
　　Through purple lips of wrath—
" What shall be done to her who dares
　　To cross your monarch's path ? "

Then spake his wily counsellors—
　　"O King of this fair land!
From distant Ind to Ethiop,
　　All bow to thy command.

" But if, before thy servants' eyes,
　　This thing they plainly see,
That Vashti doth not heed thy will
　　Nor yield herself to thee,

" The women, restive 'neath our rule,
　　Would learn to scorn our name,
And from her deed to us would come
　　Reproach and burning shame.

" Then, gracious King, sign with thy hand
　　This stern but just decree,

That Vashti lay aside her crown,
  Thy Queen no more to be."

She heard again the King's command,
  And left her high estate;
Strong in her earnest womanhood,
  She calmly met her fate,

And left the palace of the King,
  Proud of her spotless name—
A woman who could bend to grief,
  But would not bow to shame.

Thank God for Little Children.

Thank God for little children,
  Bright flowers by earth's wayside,
The dancing, joyous lifeboats
  Upon life's stormy tide.

Thank God for little children;
  When our skies are cold and gray,
They come as sunshine to our hearts,
  And charm our cares away.

I almost think the angels,
  Who tend life's garden fair,
Drop down the sweet wild blossoms
  That bloom around us here.

It seems a breath of heaven
  Round many a cradle lies,
And every little baby
  Brings a message from the skies.

Dear mothers, guard these jewels,
  As sacred offerings meet,
A wealth of household treasures
  To lay at Jesus' feet.

The Martyr of Alabama.

[The following news item appeared in the newspapers throughout the country, issue of December 27th, 1894:

" Tim Thompson, a little negro boy, was asked to dance for the amusement of some white toughs. He refused, saying he was a church member. One of the men knocked him down with a club and then danced upon his prostrate form. He then shot the boy in the hip. The boy is dead; his murderer is still at large."]

He lifted up his pleading eyes,
  And scanned each cruel face,
Where cold and brutal cowardice
  Had left its evil trace.

It was when tender memories
  Round Beth'lem's manger lay,

And mothers told their little ones
   Of Jesu's natal day.

And of the Magi from the East
   Who came their gifts to bring,
And bow in rev'rence at the feet
   Of Salem's new-born King.

And how the herald angels sang
   The choral song of peace,
That war should close his wrathful lips,
   And strife and carnage cease.

At such an hour men well may hush
   Their discord and their strife,
And o'er that manger clasp their hands
   With gifts to brighten life.

Alas! that in our favored land,
   That cruelty and crime
Should cast their shadows o'er a day,
   The fairest pearl of time.

A dark-browed boy had drawn anear
   A band of savage men,
Just as a hapless lamb might stray
   Into a tiger's den.

Cruel and dull, they saw in him
    For sport an evil chance,
And then demanded of the child
    To give to them a dance.

"Come dance for us," the rough men said;
    "I can't," the child replied,
"I cannot for the dear Lord's sake,
    Who for my sins once died."

Tho' they were strong and he was weak,
    He wouldn't his Lord deny.
His life lay in their cruel hands,
    But he for Christ could die.

Heard they aright? Did that brave child
    Their mandates dare resist?
Did he against their stern commands
    Have courage to resist?

Then recklessly a man (?) arose,
    And dealt a fearful blow.
He crushed the portals of that life,
    And laid the brave child low.

And trampled on his prostrate form,
    As on a broken toy;

Then danced with careless, brutal feet,
    Upon the murdered boy.

Christians! behold that martyred child!
    His blood cries from the ground;
Before the sleepless eye of God,
    He shows each gaping wound.

Oh! Church of Christ arise! arise!
    Lest crimson stain thy hand,
When God shall inquisition make
    For blood shed in the land.

Take sackcloth of the darkest hue,
    And shroud the pulpits round;
Servants of him who cannot lie
    Sit mourning on the ground.

Let holy horror blanch each brow,
    Pale every cheek with fears,
And rocks and stones, if ye could speak,
    Ye well might melt to tears.

Through every fane send forth a cry,
    Of sorrow and regret,
Nor in an hour of careless ease
    Thy brother's wrongs forget.

Veil not thine eyes, nor close thy lips,
   Nor speak with bated breath;
This evil shall not always last,—
   The end of it is death.

Avert the doom that crime must bring
   Upon a guilty land;
Strong in the strength that God supplies,
   For truth and justice stand.

For Christless men, with reckless hands,
   Are sowing round thy path
The tempests wild that yet shall break
   In whirlwinds of God's wrath.

THE NIGHT OF DEATH.

Twas a night of dreadful horror,—
   Death was sweeping through the land;
And the wings of dark destruction
   Were outstretched from strand to strand.

Strong men's hearts grew faint with terror,
   As the tempest and the waves

Wrecked their homes and swept them down-
    ward,
Suddenly to yawning graves.

'Mid the wastes of ruined households,
    And the tempest's wild alarms,
Stood a terror-stricken mother
    With a child within her arms.

Other children huddled 'round her,
    Each one nestling in her heart;
Swift in thought and swift in action,
    She at least from one must part.

Then she said unto her daughter,
    "Strive to save one child from death."
"Which one?" said the anxious daughter,
    As she stood with bated breath.

Oh! the anguish of that mother;
    What despair was in her eye!
All her little ones were precious;
    Which one should she leave to die?

Then outspake the brother Bennie:
    "I will take the little one."
"No," exclaimed the anxious mother;
    "No, my child, it can't be done."

"See! my boy, the waves are rising,
　　Save yourself and leave the child!"
"I will trust in Christ," he answered;
　　Grasped the little one and smiled.

Through the roar of wind and waters
　　Ever and anon she cried;
But throughout the night of terror
　　Never Bennie's voice replied.

But above the waves' wild surging
　　He had found a safe retreat,
As if God had sent an angel,
　　Just to guide his wandering feet.

When the storm had spent its fury,
　　And the sea gave up its dead,
She was mourning for her loved ones,
　　Lost amid that night of dread.

While her head was bowed in anguish,
　　On her ear there fell a voice,
Bringing surcease to her sorrow,
　　Bidding all her heart rejoice.

"Didn't I tell you true?" said Bennie,
　　And his eyes were full of light,

"When I told you God would help me
Through the dark and dreadful night?"

And he placed the little darling
 Safe within his mother's arms.
Feeling Christ had been his guardian,
 'Mid the dangers and alarms.

Oh! for faith so firm and precious,
 In the darkest, saddest night,
Till life's gloom-encircled shadows
 Fade in everlasting light.

And upon the mount of vision
 We our loved and lost shall greet,
With earth's wildest storms behind us,
 And its cares beneath our feet.

Mother's Treasures.

Two little children sit by my side,
 I call them Lily and Daffodil;
I gaze on them with a mother's pride,
 One is Edna, the other is Will.

Both have eyes of starry light,
 And laughing lips o'er teeth of pearl.

I would not change for a diadem
  My noble boy and darling girl.

To-night my heart o'erflows with joy;
  I hold them as a sacred trust;
I fain would hide them in my heart,
  Safe from tarnish of moth and rust.

What should I ask for my dear boy?
  The richest gifts of wealth or fame?
What for my girl? A loving heart
  And a fair and a spotless name?

What for my boy? That he should stand
  A pillar of strength to the state?
What for my girl? That she should be
  The friend of the poor and desolate?

I do not ask they shall never tread
  With weary feet the paths of pain.
I ask that in the darkest hour
  They may faithful and true remain.

I only ask their lives may be
  Pure as gems in the gates of pearl,
Lives to brighten and bless the world—
  This I ask for my boy and girl.

I ask to clasp their hands again
  'Mid the holy hosts of heaven,
Enraptured say: "I am here, oh! God,
"And the children Thou hast given."

The Refiner's Gold.

He stood before my heart's closed door,
  And asked to enter in;
But I had barred the passage o'er
  By unbelief and sin.

He came with nail-prints in his hands,
  To set my spirit free;
With wounded feet he trod a path
  To come and sup with me.

He found me poor and brought me gold,
  The fire of love had tried,
And garments whitened by his blood,
  My wretchedness to hide.

The glare of life had dimmed my eyes,
  Its glamour was too bright.
He came with ointment in his hands
  To heal my darkened sight.

THE REFINER'S GOLD.

He knew my heart was tempest-tossed,
    By care and pain oppressed;
He whispered to my burdened heart,
    Come unto me and rest.

He found me weary, faint and worn,
    On barren mountains cold;
With love's constraint he drew me on,
    To shelter in his fold.

Oh! foolish heart, how slow wert thou
    To welcome thy dear guest,
To change thy weariness and care
    For comfort, peace and rest.

Close to his side, oh! may I stay,
    Just to behold his face,
Till I shall wear within my soul
    The image of his grace.

The grace that changes hearts of stone
    To tenderness and love,
And bids us run with willing feet
    Unto his courts above.

A Story of the Rebellion.

The treacherous sands had caught our boat,
   And held it with a strong embrace
And death at our imprisoned crew
   Was sternly looking face to face.

With anxious hearts, but failing strength,
   We strove to push the boat from shore;
But all in vain, for there we lay
   With bated breath and useless oar.

Around us in a fearful storm
   The fiery hail fell thick and fast;
And we engirded by the sand,
   Could not return the dreadful blast.

When one arose upon whose brow
   The ardent sun had left his trace;
A noble purpose strong and high
   Uplighting all his dusky face.

Perchance within that fateful hour
   The wrongs of ages thronged apace;
But with it came the glorious hope
   Of swift deliverance to his race.

Of galling chains asunder rent,
   Of severed hearts again made one,

Of freedom crowning all the land
   Through battles gained and victories won.

"Some one," our hero firmly said,
   "Must die to get us out of this;"
Then leaped upon the strand and bared
   His bosom to the bullets' hiss.

"But ye are soldiers, and can fight,
   May win in battles yet unfought;
I have no offering but my life,
   And if they kill me it is nought."

With steady hands he grasped the boat,
   And boldly pushed it from the shore;
Then fell by rebel bullets pierced,
   His life work grandly, nobly o'er.

Our boat was rescued from the sands
   And launched in safety on the tide;
But he our comrade good and grand,
   In our defence had bravely died.

BURIAL OF SARAH.

He stood before the sons of Heth,
   And bowed his sorrowing head;

"I've come," he said, "to buy a place
    Where I may lay my dead.

"I am a stranger in your land,
    My home has lost its light;
Grant me a place where I may lay
    My dead away from sight."

Then tenderly the sons of Heth
    Gazed on the mourner's face,
And said, "Oh, Prince, amid our dead,
    Choose thou her resting-place.

"The sepulchres of those we love,
    We place at thy command;
Against the plea thy grief hath made
    We close not heart nor hand."

The patriarch rose and bowed his head,
    And said, "One place I crave;
'Tis at the end of Ephron's field,
    And called Machpelah's cave.

"Entreat him that he sell to me
    For her last sleep that cave;
I do not ask for her I loved
    The freedom of a grave."

The son of Zohar answered him,
  "Hearken, my lord. to me;
Before our sons, the field and cave
  I freely give to thee."

"I will not take it as a gift,"
  The grand old man then said;
"I pray thee let me buy the place
  Where I may lay my dead."

And with the promise in his heart,
  His seed should own that land.
He gave the shekels for the field
  He took from Ephron's hand.

And saw afar the glorious day
  His chosen seed should tread,
The soil where he in sorrow lay
  His loved and cherished dead.

Going East.

She came from the East a fair. young bride,
  With a light and a bounding heart,
To find in the distant West a home
  With her husband to make a start.

He builded his cabin far away,
  Where the prairie flower bloomed wild;
Her love made lighter all his toil,
  And joy and hope around him smiled.

She plied her hands to life's homely tasks,
  And helped to build his fortunes up;
While joy and grief, like bitter and sweet,
  Were mingled and mixed in her cup.

He sowed in his fields of golden grain,
  All the strength of his manly prime;
Nor music of birds, nor brooks, nor bees,
  Was as sweet as the dollar's chime.

She toiled and waited through weary years
  For the fortune that came at length;
But toil and care and hope deferred,
  Had stolen and wasted her strength.

The cabin changed to a stately home,
  Rich carpets were hushing her tread;
But light was fading from her eye,
  And the bloom from her cheek had fled.

Slower and heavier grew her step,
  While his gold and his gains increased;

But his proud domain had not the charm
   Of her humble home in the East.

Within her eye was a restless light,
   And a yearning that never ceased,
A longing to see the dear old home
   She had left in the distant East.

A longing to clasp her mother's hand,
   And nestle close to her heart,
And to feel the heavy cares of life
   Like the sun-kissed shadows depart.

Her husband was adding field to field,
   And new wealth to his golden store;
And little thought the shadow of death
   Was entering in at his door.

He had no line to sound the depths
   Of her tears repressed and unshed;
Nor dreamed 'mid plenty a human heart
   Could be starving, but not for bread.

The hungry heart was stilled at last;
   Its restless, baffled yearning ceased.
A lonely man sat by the bier
   Of a corpse that was going East.

The Hermit's Sacrifice.

From Rome's palaces and villas
    Gaily issued forth a throng;
From her humbler habitations
    Moved a human tide along.

Haughty dames and blooming maidens,
    Men who knew not mercy's sway,
Thronged into the Coliseum
    On that Roman holiday.

From the lonely wilds of Asia,
    From her jungles far away,
From the distant torrid regions,
    Rome had gathered beasts of prey.

Lions restless, roaring, rampant,
    Tigers with their stealthy tread,
Leopards bright, and fierce, and fiery,
    Met in conflict wild and dread.

Fierce and fearful was the carnage
    Of the maddened beasts of prey,
As they fought and rent each other
    Urged by men more fierce than they.

Till like muffled thunders breaking
    On a vast and distant shore,

THE HERMIT'S SACRIFICE.

Fainter grew the yells of tigers,
   And the lions' dreadful roar.

On the crimson-stained arena
   Lay the victims of the fight;
Eyes which once had glared with anguish,
   Lost in death their baleful light.

Then uprose the gladiators
   Armed for conflict unto death,
Waiting for the prefect's signal,
   Cold and stern with bated breath.

" Ave Cæsar, morituri,
   Te, salutant," rose the cry
From the lips of men ill-fated,
   Doomed to suffer and to die.

Then began the dreadful contest,
   Lives like chaff were thrown away,
Rome with all her pride and power
   Butchered for a holiday.

Eagerly the crowd were waiting,
   Loud the clashing sabres rang;
When between the gladiators
   All unarmed a hermit sprang.

"Cease your bloodshed," cried the hermit,
  "On this carnage place your ban;"
But with flashing swords they answered,
  "Back unto your place, old man."

From their path the gladiators
  Thrust the strange intruder back,
Who between their hosts advancing
  Calmly parried their attack.

All undaunted by their weapons,
  Stood the old heroic man;
While a maddened cry of anger
  Through the vast assembly ran.

"Down with him," cried out the people,
  As with thumbs unbent they glared,
Till the prefect gave the signal
  That his life should not be spared.

Men grew wild with wrathful passion,
  When his fearless words were said
Cruelly they fiercely showered
  Stones on his devoted head.

Bruised and bleeding fell the hermit,
  Victor in that hour of strife;

Gaining in his death a triumph
  That he could not win in life.

Had he uttered on the forum
  Struggling thoughts within him born,
Men had jeered his words as madness,
  But his deed they could not scorn.

Not in vain had been his courage,
  Nor for naught his daring deed;
From his grave his mangled body
  Did for wretched captives plead.

From that hour Rome, grown more thoughtful,
  Ceased her sport in human gore;
And into her Coliseum
  Gladiators came no more.

Songs for the People.

Let me make the songs for the people,
  Songs for the old and young;
Songs to stir like a battle-cry
  Wherever they are sung.

Not for the clashing of sabres,
  For carnage nor for strife;

But songs to thrill the hearts of men
  With more abundant life.

Let me make the songs for the weary,
  Amid life's fever and fret,
Till hearts shall relax their tension,
  And careworn brows forget.

Let me sing for little children,
  Before their footsteps stray,
Sweet anthems of love and duty,
  To float o'er life's highway

I would sing for the poor and aged,
  When shadows dim their sight;
Of the bright and restful mansions,
  Where there shall be no night.

Our world, so worn and weary,
  Needs music, pure and strong,
To hush the jangle and discords
  Of sorrow, pain, and wrong.

Music to soothe all its sorrow,
  Till war and crime shall cease;
And the hearts of men grown tender
  Girdle the world with peace.

Let the Light Enter.

The dying words of Goethe.

"Light! more light! the shadows deepen,
  And my life is ebbing low,
Throw the windows widely open:
  Light! more light! before I go.

"Softly let the balmy sunshine
  Play around my dying bed,
E'er the dimly lighted valley
  I with lonely feet must tread.

"Light! more light! for Death is weaving
  Shadows 'round my waning sight,
And I fain would gaze upon him
  Through a stream of earthly light."

Not for greater gifts of genius;
  Not for thoughts more grandly bright,
All the dying poet whispers
  Is a prayer for light, more light.

Heeds he not the gathered laurels,
  Fading slowly from his sight;
All the poet's aspirations
  Centre in that prayer for light.

Gracious Saviour, when life's day-dreams
  Melt and vanish from the sight,
May our dim and longing vision
  Then be blessed with light, more light.

An Appeal to My Countrywomen.

You can sigh o'er the sad-eyed Armenian
  Who weeps in her desolate home.
You can mourn o'er the exile of Russia
  From kindred and friends doomed to roam.

You can pity the men who have woven
  From passion and appetite chains
To coil with a terrible tension
  Around their heartstrings and brains.

You can sorrow o'er little children
  Disinherited from their birth,
The wee waifs and toddlers neglected,
  Robbed of sunshine, music and mirth.

For beasts you have gentle compassion;
  Your mercy and pity they share.
For the wretched, outcast and fallen
  You have tenderness, love and care.

But hark! from our Southland are floating
   Sobs of anguish, murmurs of pain,
And women heart-stricken are weeping
   Over their tortured and their slain.

On their brows the sun has left traces;
   Shrink not from their sorrow in scorn.
When they entered the threshold of being
   The children of a King were born.

Each comes as a guest to the table
   The hand of our God has outspread,
To fountains that ever leap upward,
   To share in the soil we all tread.

When ye plead for the wrecked and fallen,
   The exile from far-distant shores,
Remember that men are still wasting
   Life's crimson around your own doors.

Have ye not, oh, my favored sisters,
   Just a plea, a prayer or a tear,
For mothers who dwell 'neath the shadows
   Of agony, hatred and fear?

Men may tread down the poor and lowly,
   May crush them in anger and hate,

But surely the mills of God's justice
    Will grind out the grist of their fate.

Oh, people sin-laden and guilty,
    So lusty and proud in your prime,
The sharp sickles of God's retribution
    Will gather your harvest of crime.

Weep not, oh my well-sheltered sisters,
    Weep not for the Negro alone,
But weep for your sons who must gather
    The crops which their fathers have sown.

Go read on the tombstones of nations
    Of chieftains who masterful trod,
The sentence which time has engraven,
    That they had forgotten their God.

'Tis the judgment of God that men reap
    The tares which in madness they sow,
Sorrow follows the footsteps of crime,
    And Sin is the consort of Woe.

FRANCES E. W HARPER.

www.ingramcontent.com/pod-product-compliance
Lightning Source LLC
Chambersburg PA
CBHW020331090426
42735CB00009B/1493